Apollo's Computers

Patrick H. Stakem

(c) 2014, 2022

Table of Contents

Introduction..3

Author...4

Saturn-I...6

Saturn-V vehicle...9

    First stage - S1C..15

    Second stage - S-II...17

    Third stage – S-IVB...18

    IU...18

    LVDC 21

Apollo payload..25

    LES...25

    Command Module..26

        AGC...26

        Service Module..32

        LEM..35

Launch Support...37

    VAB..37

    Launch Complex 39..39

        The Launch Control Center 40

        Checkout and Launch Control Computers..................41

    Mission Control Center (MCC) at JSC..............................43

    Tracking system network...47

The Skylab Missions...49

Manufacturer's Sites..50

Afterword...56

Glossary..57

References...62

If you enjoyed this book, you might also be interested in some of
these..73

Introduction

Apollo was built in the era of "big iron" computer mainframes. The concept of an onboard computer for space missions was radically new. There was only one place in the world that could design the Apollo Guidance Computers, and that was MIT. It took most of the U.S.'s production of integrated circuits, another radical idea replacing individual vacuum tubes, to build the AGC's. It took 2,000 person-years of independent code review and validation to ensure that they would operate properly.

Besides the technical challenges, the Apollo missions were a matter of National Prestige. In the Space Race between the United States and the Soviet Union, President Kennedy said we were going to the Moon and return safely before the end of the (1960's) decade, so we did.

The flight computers for the Saturn launch vehicle were an evolution of earlier missile guidance efforts. The massive Saturn-V first stage was built from clustered Jupiter rockets. The earlier and smaller Saturn-I was built of clustered Redstone rockets, which were themselves a derivative of the early German V-2 rockets by the Von Braun Team. The Saturn's upper stages were all new technology, using liquid hydrogen and oxygen. The vehicle had to achieve and maintain a precise trajectory from its launch site in Florida, to lunar orbit, to the lunar surface and back, and then return to Earth. All this took unprecedented computing power.

This book is a brief synopsis of the architecture and applications of the Apollo computers. There is a lot of archived material on the topic, and the list of references in this book is a good starting point. The amazing thing is, the first computer on another world was designed and built before computers were commodity items. It worked as planned. Although your phone has more computing power than the entire Saturn vehicle, you shouldn't trust it to get you to the moon and back.

In this document, you will see both English and Metric (SI) units, as used in the referenced documents. By 1970, NASA had a requirement to use SI units exclusively, but this was frequently waived. This policy eventually lead to the loss of the Mars Climate Orbiter mission in September of 1999.

Author

Mr. Stakem has been interested in rockets and spacecraft since high school. He received a Bachelor's degree in Electrical Engineering from Carnegie-Mellon University in 1971, where he was a member of the Applied Space Sciences group. His first job was for Fairchild Industries, then building the ATS-6 spacecraft. Wernher von Braun joined Fairchild as Vice-President of Engineering during this time, so, technically, Mr. Stakem was once a member of the von Braun Team. Specializing in support of spacecraft onboard computers, he has worked at every NASA Center. He supported the Apollo-Soyuz mission with the ATS-6 communications satellite. He received Master's degrees in Physics and Computer Science from the Johns Hopkins University. He has taught for Loyola University in Maryland, Graduate Department of Computer Science, AIAA, The Johns Hopkins University, Whiting School of Engineering, and Capitol Technology University.

It is worth noting that the author has extensive hands-on experience with IBM mainframes, including the 7040, 7090, and the System S/360 that ran Mission Control. He is conversant in both Fortran-G and Fortran-H, and is moderately competent with Job Control Language (JCL). He can load tapes, put paper in the line printer, and read AND punch decks of cards.

Cover photo:

The business end of a Saturn Rocket on display at Marshall Space Flight Center, picture by the author.

Saturn-I

Saturn-I was the heavy lift vehicle developed for the Apollo Program. It used a cluster of older-technology Redstone rockets. It was used for flight verification of Apollo hardware, but could only boost payloads to Earth orbit. Ten Saturn-I's were flown, and an advanced follow-on version, the Saturn-Ib, had a more powerful upper stage. The first stage, the S-I, was developed by Chrysler Corporation, with the upper stages built by Douglas and Convair. It stood some 180 feet tall, and weighted over 1.1 million pounds. It could put a payload of 20,000 pounds in Earth orbit.

The Block-1 vehicles, 1-4, were guided by an Instrument Unit (IU) atop the S-1 stage This included the Ford ST-90 stabilized platform. The early vehicles simply followed a pre-defined ballistic trajectory. Block-II vehicles used an IBM ASC-15 flight computer. The four outermost rocket engines were gimbaled, for flight control.

The Instrument Unit (IU) was introduced with unit SA-5, and used on the subsequent flights SA-6 through SA-10. These were designed at MSFC, and used for vehicle guidance, control, and sequencing, after the first stage completed its work. The IU's had their own telemetry, tracking, and power systems. The first model was a pressurized ring structure 154 inches in diameter, and 58 inches high. The large diameter matched the profile of the launch vehicle. Version two of the Instrument Unit was used on the Pegasus missions, SA-8, -9, and -10. This version was only 34 inches high and 21 feet in diameter. It was constructed of an aluminum honeycomb, less than an inch thick, and weighed 2,670 pounds. It was unpressurized, unlike the previous version. Subsequent Saturn-V vehicles used a third version. The IU was placed between the S-IV B second stage and the Apollo spacecraft payload. The IU was cooled by a water/methanol heat exchanger, and powered by batteries.

The IU held the IBM LVDC digital computer, an analog computer for vehicle flight control, the ST-124 inertial guidance platform, accelerometers, and gyros. The sensor platform was a derivative of the one used in the V-2. The analog control computer took measurements of angular changes and lateral acceleration, and commanded the engine gimbals to adjust accordingly.

The ASC-15 Launch Vehicle Digital Computer was developed by IBM Corporation for the Titan missile. A modified version was used on the Saturn I Block-II. The computer used inputs from the ST-124 inertial platform to calculate trajectory and navigation. The processor was serial, using fixed-point data of a 28-bit word size. The hardware was built from modules containing discrete components. Previous versions of the Saturn had used open loop control, with a carefully timed sequence of events. A preprogrammed sequence, depending only on time, used a 6-track magnetic tape recorder and sets of relays. The addition of the ASC-15 allowed closed-loop control for adaptive path guidance. The control update rate was 25 times per second. The computer clock was 2.048 MHz. The memory was up to 32 kilobytes of 28-bit words. Within these 28 bits were a 26-bit sign-magnitude data word, with two bits of error detection. Instructions were 13 bits long, with parity. Two instructions were packed in a memory word. Instructions had a 4-bit operation code, and a 9-bit address field. Memory used magnetic core technology, with delay lines for temporary storage. A separate hardware multiply and divide unit was included. Add time was 82 microseconds, multiply 328, and divide 656. The instruction rate was around 12,000 per second. The complexity of the unit was equivalent to over 40,000 transistors. It weighed 75 pounds, and required about 150 watts of power. It was programmed in assembly language.

The computer system also did pre-launch self-test and supported mission simulation. Its primary purpose was booster guidance. In mission SA-6, one engine shut down prematurely, but the computer automatically adjusted the trajectory to compensate properly. 28-vdc power was supplied from alkaline silver-zinc battery packs, and the computer required four different voltage sources.

The digital computer had an associated Launch Vehicle Data Adapter (LVDA), which was an interface to the inertial platform, the command receiver and telemetry transmitters, the ground checkout computer (while on the launch pad), and other vehicle sensors, such as separation switches. The LVDA provided analog to digital conversion. It communicated with the LVDC over a 512 kbps serial interface. The LVDA input link from the RCA–110 ground computer was over a 14-bit data line. The LVDA weighed 214 pounds, and required 320 watts of power. Local storage of data in the LVDA was via glass delay lines. The LVDA had the ability to interrupt the LVDC.

After the vehicle was launched and cleared the tower, a stored program in the Launch Vehicle Digital Computer (LVDC) commanded the vehicle to roll about its long axis, and then to pitch to the desired azimuth. The sequence of events was controlled by a series of pulses on a 6-track tape recorder. These were pre-programmed values, based on ground calculations. The IU also controlled the time of the first stage engine cut-off and staging. This was based on a predetermined value of fuel in the tanks. This was essentially the same guidance system approach used in the V-2 rocket. Guidance during second stage burn also depended on a time sequence, but employed closed-loop adaptive guidance as well.

Saturn-V vehicle

The story of the Saturn rocket is the story of liquid-fueled rocket development, starting in World War-2 Germany. After the war, it was continued both in the United States and the Soviet Union by members of the German teams. The driver was now not war, but political and world prestige. The story of the Saturn-V moon rocket starts with the V-2 missile development and continues through the Redstone, Jupiter, and the Saturn-1 rockets.

The first ballistic missile, the German V-2, relied on being launched from a precisely surveyed location, on a fixed heading, with an exact burn time. During powered flight, an analog servo system would adjust for deviations from that path. After the engine was shut down, the trajectory was fixed.

The German V-2 Field Operations Manual was captured by US forces along with missiles and launch and ground support equipment. The manual was translated at the Army's Aberdeen Proving Grounds (MD). It tells the ground troops how to launch the missile. The manual assumes a high school education. After the launch site is accurately surveyed, the missile was erected and fueled. Then, the troops were instructed to "…point fin number 1 towards London…" The distance was set into the timer that would shut down the engine, and the missile was launched as the support equipment made a hasty withdrawal to avoid Allied air power. This approach was used by Iraq during the First Gulf War. By then, the U.S had anti-missile capacity.

There was not much progress when the intercontinental missiles of the early Cold War period came along. The early missile guidance computers were located in underground bunkers, and transmitted their steering commands to the missile via a radio link. The missiles went ballistic after the engine burned out, a period of several minutes. After that, the laws of physics took over. No control or adjustments were possible after burn-out.

In the 1960's, missile guidance computers were developed that could adjust the trajectory after launch, but only during powered flight. These included the Univac *Athena* computer for the Air Force's Titan missile system, and the Burroughs *Mod 1* for the Atlas missile system. The Smithsonian Institution has one of each computer.

The development of onboard missile guidance computers was driven by the need to launch from submarines. Since the launch is not taking place from a pre-surveyed location, the calculations are more difficult. The exact position of the submarine must be known. This led to the development by the Navy of the Transit system, an early predecessor of the GPS (Global Positing System). The Transit system relied on a series of Navigation Satellites in known orbits. Once you launch the guidance computer, it only has to work for several minutes, and is not reused.

The early manned missions such as Project Mercury, were basically "a man in a can" atop a ballistic missile, and did not incorporate computing power. After the manned Mercury missions, the crew, drawn from the military test pilot world, demanded some input in flying the vehicle. The Gemini spacecraft carried a small computer to enable rendezvous and docking with an Agena target vehicle, a skill that would be needed for the later Apollo missions to the moon. Gemini, designed for rendezvous, had a computer that could actually take over from the Titan launch vehicle computer. The crew could then fly the vehicle into orbit.

The Gemini Guidance computer, built by IBM, weighted 59 pounds. It had 16 machine language instructions, with a 140 millisecond ADD time. Equations were verified at the Fortran language level. Auxiliary tape memory was used (on Gemini VIII and later) and glass delay line registers were used for temporary storage.

The Saturn-1 launch vehicle used a unique control computer built from discrete components, with 27-bit words. A magnetic drum of less than 100k words capacity, was used as memory. It was a simplex design, with no redundancy. It weighed under 100 pounds, and consumed 275 watts of power.

The Saturn vehicles were developed by the von Braun team at Marshall Space Flight Center, formally the Army's Redstone Arsenal, in Huntsville, Alabama. Von Braun and his team of scientists and engineers had been brought to the U.S. by the Army after World War II ended. The rocket program was kicked off during the early post-World War-II Cold War era by President Eisenhower. At the time, the United States was in a race to space, and particularly, a launch vehicle race, with the Soviet Union. Each U. S. military service, the Army, Navy, and Air Force were developing their own rockets. Inter-service rivalry was finally squashed by Secretary of

Defense Charles Wilson, who decided in November of 1956 to make the Air Force the primary missile developer for long range ballistic and space missions. The specifications for a heavy-lift vehicle were developed by the Advanced Research Projects Agency (ARPA).

The Army found a loophole in Wilson's decision. His edict applied to weapons systems, so the Army Ballistic Missile Agency (ABMA), founded in 1956 at the Redstone Arsenal, decided to pursue non-military space launches. The only way to achieve the heavy lift required was to use a cluster of proven, off-the-shelf engines, from earlier vehicles like the Redstone and Jupiter. These rockets had also been developed by the von Braun team at ABMA. The "Super-Jupiter" (Saturn) solved the Stage-1, getting-off-the-ground, problem in an evolutionary fashion, building upon proven components, designs, and procedures. The Russians proceeded along the same path, using clustering techniques on their Soyuz launch vehicle, which was derived from an earlier military missile.

The formation of the National Aerospace Administration (NASA) in 1958 for pursuing peaceful civilian uses of space provided a framework to address the lunar mission, a high-visibility project to demonstrate the superiority of American technology to the world, kicked off by President Kennedy.

President Kennedy said the Saturn-I represented the first time the U. S. lift capability to orbit exceeded that of the Soviets, in a speech at Brooks AFB in San Antonio, Texas. He was assassinated in Dallas the next day, and did not get to see his project completed. The Saturn represented one of the first launch vehicles not to be designed specifically for military purposes. As a follow-on to the previous Jupiter rocket, and since Saturn is the next planet beyond Jupiter in the solar system, it got its name. There was no follow-on heavy lift vehicle beyond Saturn, as NASA chose to develop the mostly-reusable Space Transportation System (Shuttle).

As part of the development of the Saturn-V moon rocket, the Saturn-I vehicle was developed. There were a series of ten successful flights of this vehicle. The second stage of Saturn-I became the Saturn-V's third stage, and a new massive booster was developed for the first stage.

The Saturn-V was a three-stage, human-rated launch vehicle. Thirteen of the vehicles were launched, with never a loss of crew. Saturn-V models are on display at Marshall Space Flight Center in Huntsville, Alabama, the Johnson space Center, in Houston, Texas, and at the Kennedy Space flight Center in Florida. These are flight models, never used. All three stages used the same oxidizer, liquid oxygen (LOX). The first stage used RP-1 fuel, and the second and third stages used liquid hydrogen, LH2.

The vehicle stood some 363 feet tall, from the launch pad to the Apollo Capsule. It weighed a mere 6.5 million pounds, ready to launch. It could lift over a quarter of a million pounds to Earth orbit.

First stage - S1C

The first stage of the Saturn Rocket "stack" was the heavy lift stage, consisting of five Rocketdyne F-1 engines, one fixed in the middle, and four outside units that could swivel for steering and attitude adjustment. The first stage booster did not incorporate active guidance. The stage's job was to get the rocket and its payload from a standing start to 67 kilometers up, 93 kilometers downrange, and moving at 2,300 meters per second. That required 168 seconds of engine burn time. The total thrust developed by the engines was 7,600,000 pounds-force. Most of the first stage was fuel. The dry weight was about 130 tons, and the fueled weight was 2,300 tons. Any deviation of the vehicle during first stage burn was noted, and adjusted for during the second stage burn.

The engine's sequence of events was controlled by an onboard sequencer. This was not a computer, but just a fixed series of commands that were played out in time sequence. The center engine of the stage was started 8.9 seconds before launch, with pairs of outboard engines starting at 300 millisecond intervals. This technique was used to reduce structural loading on the rocket. When the computer in the Instrument Unit confirmed thrust level correctness, the pad hold-down arms released the rocket.

In the Instrument Unit, the Saturn Emergency Detection System (EDS) inhibited engine shutdown for 30 seconds after launch. It was calculated that this was safer than having a shutdown early in the sequence, which would result in a non-survivable event for the astronauts.

The sequencing of events took place on a prearranged timeline. As the vehicle lifted past the tower, it was yawed 1.25 degrees away from the tower, to provide a margin of safety in high winds. Past 400 feet, a pitch program kicked in, having been adjusted for the expected winds that month. The vehicle also rolled to the correct flight azimuth. The outboard engines were tilted to the outside, so their thrust vectors went through the vehicles center of gravity. This was to minimize the effect of one outboard engine failing. At roughly 1 minute into the flight, the vehicle broke the sound barrier. Guidance adjustment was provided by the computer in the Instrument Unit (IU). The initial trajectory was designed to gain altitude quickly as the main goal. The engines; thrust grew from 7.5 million pounds-force at launch to over 9 million, in the thinner air. At the same time, the mass of the vehicle went down dramatically, as fuel and oxidizer was burned at the rate of 13 tons per second. The maximum acceleration was reached in over two minutes, at 4 G's. At this point, the center engine was shut down to limit acceleration, and the four outer engines used the remaining fuel and oxidizer. When oxidizer or fuel depletion was sensed at the pumps, the first stage was separated from the vehicle. Up high and moving fast, the first stage was separated, and the rest of the vehicle headed for Earth orbit.

Second stage - S-II

The second stage of the Saturn-V used the new J-2 rocket engines, burning liquid hydrogen and liquid oxygen. This stage was also almost completely fuel, weighing about 40 tons dry, and over 500 tons fueled. The engines developed over a million pounds-force in vacuum. The difference between the temperature of the propellant and the oxidizer was significant, around 70 degrees C. Thus, the liquid oxygen, being hotter, tried to boil the liquid hydrogen. This was prevented by extensive insulation.

After the first stage separation was confirmed, the second stage was ignited by the controller in the IU, and burned for about six minutes. By that time, the vehicle was 110 miles up, and nearly at orbital velocity. The second stage was actively controlled during power flight by the computer in the IU, using a path-adaptive guidance plan, that optimized propellant usage. Every two seconds, the actual state vector was compared to the expected. Commands could be issued by the digital computer to the analog flight controller computer (in the IU) to command gimbal angle changes in the nozzles, for steering control. The IU was also monitoring propellant levels in the S-II stage, and commanded engine shutdown and stage separation at the right time.

About 38 seconds after second stage ignition, the vehicle control switched from a preprogrammed trajectory to closed loop control. The Instrument Unit now computed in real time the most fuel-efficient trajectory toward its target orbit. If the Instrument Unit failed, the crew could switch control of the Saturn to the Command Module's computer, take manual control, or abort the flight.

Third stage – S-IVB

This stage had a single J-2 engine using liquid hydrogen and oxygen, and weighed around 11 tons dry, 130 tons fueled. This engine was a derivative of the one used as the second stage of the earlier Saturn-1 vehicle. The new engine was restartable once. This was used to get to Earth orbit, and then to enter the trans-lunar injection path to lunar orbit. Active guidance continued by the Instrument Unit.

IU

The Instrument Unit (IU) was the center point of the data flow on the Saturn vehicle, seeing data both up and down the vehicle. It was introduced with the Saturn-I, Block–II, unit SA-5. It was designed at MSFC, and produced by IBM Corp. It used for vehicle guidance, control, and sequencing. The IU had its own telemetry, tracking, and power systems. Subsequent Saturn-V vehicles used a third version. The IU was placed between the S-IVB second stage and the Apollo spacecraft payload, and was an integral structural member.

In addition to the digital computer, the IU had an analog Flight Control Computer. The digital unit monitored status and calculated attitude corrections. The analog computer was used to command these corrections as angular adjustments for the swiveling nozzles.

The unit was powered by four 28-volt batteries. Heat generation in the unit was handled by a liquid cooling loop, which dumped heat to the outside air.

Before launch, a precision theodolite was used to align the inertial platform in the IU to the exact launch azimuth. The ST-124 inertial platform switched from an Earth Reference to a space-based frame of reference 5 seconds before liftoff.

The ST-124 3-degrees-of-freedom Inertial Platform Assembly, produced by Bendix Corporation, was a derivative of similar gyro-based platforms used on the German V-2 missile. It included three single degree of freedom precision gyros, and accelerometers. Active guidance was not required during the main boost phase, as the pre-programmed first stage's job was to just get the vehicle up and moving.

The IU included a data adapter to interface with the various sensors and other systems. This unit transformed the various formats, including analog, to a standard digital format the digital computer could use.

Before launch, the LVDC was connected to the ground control computer via umbilical.

Control of the first stage was based only on a time sequence. True guidance was not applied until after the second stage burn had been initiated. Engine cut-off was determined by having achieved a velocity sufficient to enter Earth orbit. The algorithm was a minimum propellant flight path, using calculus of variations. For the second and subsequent stages, closed loop control was used.

When the IU sensed that the propellant level in the first stage had reached a preprogrammed value, it commanded stage cut-off and the separation sequence. It handled a similar role for the second stage. The IU controlled the first burn of the third stage, to achieve Earth orbit, and the second burn, to enter the trans-lunar trajectory. The IU had done its job at this point, about 6 ½ hours after launch.

Until a large enough aircraft became available, the IU was delivered from Huntsville to the Cape via barge. In one case, schedule pressure required construction of a portable clean room on the barge, and work on the IU was completed en route.

A flight spare IU can be seen at the National Air and Space Museum, Steven F. Udvar-Hazy Center, near Dulles Airport in Virginia.

LVDC

The LVDC in the Instrument Unit was developed by IBM Corporation. It was used on the Saturn I Block-II and Saturn-V. The computer used inputs from the ST-124 inertial platform to calculate trajectory and navigation. The processor was serial, using fixed-point data of a 28-bit word size. The hardware was built up from modules containing discrete components. There were two arithmetic logic units (ALU's), one for addition, subtraction, and logical operations, and the other for multiply and divide. These could operate independently. The CPU included the two ALU units, and a set of registers to hold data. The serial registers were implemented as ultrasonic glass delay lines.

The computer clock was 2.048 MHz, and an instruction cycle took 82 microseconds. Most instructions used a single cycle, but the longest one took 5 cycles. The memory was 32 kilobytes of 28-bit words. Within these 28 bits were 26-bit sign-magnitude data words, with two bits of error detection. Instructions were 13 bits long, with parity. Two instructions were packed into a memory word. Instructions had a 4-bit operation code, and a 9-bit address field. There were 18 instructions in the instruction set. Add time was 82 microseconds, multiply 328, and divide 656. The complexity of the unit was equivalent to over 40,000 transistors. It could achieve and instruction execution rate of just over 12,000 instructions per second. The computer weighed 75 pounds, and required 150 watts of power.

There was some early discussion of replacing the AGC with an LVDC, but this was not pursued.

Memory used magnetic core technology, with delay lines for temporary storage. It featured serial read. A maximum of eight modules of 4096 bits each could be used.

Upon RESET, the CPU fetched the starting address from memory address zero. This was used as an operand for an unconditional jump ("HOP") instruction. There were specific I/O instructions. The machine was programmed in its assembly language. No source code examples still exist. There is some evidence that the program was originally produced by engineers in Fortran, which would make sense, because it could be run as a simulation. The Fortran was then hand-assembled into LVDC code.

The circuitry was triple-modularly-redundant (TMR) with voting (using disagreement registers), and, in some critical cases, quadruple redundant. The triple seven-stage instruction execution pipelines had voting circuitry at each stage. The published reliability number was 99.6% over 250 hours of operation, although the unit was only required to operate for minutes in the early launches. There were 11 hardware interrupts on the early Saturn I-B models, including one for engine cut-off. The LVDA unit also served as the interrupt controller, receiving all the interrupts from external devices, and signaling the CPU over a single line. Interrupts could be masked (ignored).

The digital computer had an associated Launch Vehicle Data Adapter (LVDA), which was an I/O interface to the inertial platform, the command receiver and telemetry transmitters, the RCA-110 ground checkout computer (while on the launch pad), and other vehicle sensors, such as separation switches. The LVDA also provided analog-to -digital conversion. It communicated with the LVDC over a 512 kbps serial interface. The LVDA input link from the RCA–110 ground computer was a 14-bit data line. The LVDA weighed 214 pounds, and required 320 watts of power. Local storage of data in the LVDA was via glass delay lines

The LVDC and the associated LVDA was a real-time control computer. Previous versions of the Saturn had used open loop control, with a carefully timed sequence of events.

The LVDC computer system also did pre-launch self-test and supported mission simulation. Its primary purpose was booster guidance. In mission SA-6, one engine shut down prematurely, but the computer automatically adjusted the trajectory to compensate properly. 28 vdc power was supplied from alkaline silver-zinc battery packs

ST-124-M Inertial Platform Assembly

The ST-124-M enabled closed loop guidance control for the entire powered flight. It was built by the Bendix Corporation. It included 3 integrating accelerometers, and a 3-gimbal gyro.

"The ST-124 platform is a four-gimbal system which permitted full freedom about all three vehicle axes. The gimbal order from the vehicle to the inner gimbal is pitch redundant, yaw, pitch limited, and roll. The pitch redundant gimbal is positioned from a pitch command resolver and a gimbal resolver operating into an associated gimbal servo. The pitch limited gimbal is controlled to essentially zero (steady state). Three pendulous integrating gyro accelerometers are mounted on the ST-124 stabilized element. The range and cross range accelerometers are normal to each other in the local horizontal plane at launch with the range accelerometer directed down range. Cross range output is positive right with the observer facing down range. The altitude accelerometer is directed up and normal to the launch horizontal plane. The ST-124 platform is stabilized by three air bearing, single-degree-of-freedom gyros mounted with the sensitive axes mutually perpendicular. The gyro axes (sensitive or input, output, spin reference) are oriented such that some of the "g"-sensitive drifts a are effectively zero or, in any case, a minimum."

The Flight Control computer in the IU was an analog machine. It took computed attitude correction commands from the LDVC and attitude state data from the ST-124-M. It commanded the roll control for the first stage, and pitch, roll, and yaw control for Stages 2 and 3.

Apollo payload

The payload consisted of the Launch Escape System, the Apollo capsule, the service module, and the lunar lander. The launch escape system (LES) was located above the Apollo capsule and was jettisoned early in flight. The Lunar Excursion Module (LEM) was stored behind the service module. Once in Earth orbit, the capsule and Service Module were separated, the capsule rotated 180 degrees, and docked to the Lunar module. The lunar package was then separated from the third stage. The capsule, lander, and service module left Earth orbit heading for the moon, while the Third stage was commanded into a solar orbit, to get it out of the way.

LES

The Launch Escape System would pull the Apollo capsule away from the launch vehicle in case of an emergency on the pad, or a booster failure. It was jettisoned about 30 seconds after liftoff. It was never needed during an Apollo flight, but had been tested twice in Pad Abort tests, with boilerplate capsules, and tested five times in-air, using the Little Joe launch system and engineering model capsules, at the White Sands Missile range.

The system could be activated by the Mission Commander in the capsule, or by a break in two of the three wires that ran down the length of the launch vehicle. The LES used solid propellant motors.

The LES had eight pressure sensing pitot tubes similar to those used in aircraft. These sensors were monitored by the launch vehicle guidance computer and the AGC in the Command Modules. The LES did not incorporate its own computer.

Command Module

The Command Module, or Apollo capsule, was the cockpit and living quarters for the three astronauts. The computing heart of the capsule was the unique Apollo Guidance Computer. The need for a computer onboard the Apollo was required by the chosen approach to the mission, lunar-orbit rendezvous. Part of the spacecraft (Command Module) would remain in lunar orbit, while a detachable part (LEM) would descend to the surface. Later, the LEM would return to lunar orbit and rendezvous with the Command Module, which would then leave lunar orbit and return to Earth. The ability of the Command Module and LEM to do in-flight computations was crucial to this approach. At the time, the only guidance computers were developed for ballistic missiles.

AGC

The Apollo Guidance Computer (AGC) was developed by the MIT Instrumentation Lab, headed by Charles Stark Draper, based on the Polaris submarine-launched missile guidance computers. The Project kicked off in 1961 with a 1-page specification from NASA. The unit was designed at MIT, and was built by Raytheon

Missiles and Space Division. This was an overwhelmingly difficult task, with the state of the technology at the time. The integrated circuit had been invented only 2 years earlier. The early model computer used a core-transistor logic, and later models used a single type of NOR integrated circuit after October 1962. A prototype was built in 4 racks, each the size of modern refrigerators. Using a single type of integrated circuit building block simplified the procurement of parts, which were supplied by Fairchild Semiconductor and Signetics. An approach for in-flight repair by the astronauts for the guidance computer en-route to the moon was considered. A soldering iron was to be included in the Apollo capsule. Later, the reliability of the unit precluded this approach. The tricky part was re-packaging the four floor to ceiling racks of circuitry into a small box. A simple matter of detail.

Before an actual AGC had been implemented, simulations were run on the Lab's Honeywell 1800, or IBM 360 computers. The simulations ran about 10 times slower than real time.

Since a single type of logic gate was used, these could be combined on a logic board that held 60 circuits. These boards were also used in the construction of simulators and test equipment for the computers. Initial delivery of a computer to MIT took place in August of 1964. Ten more units were under construction at Raytheon. They were delivered late, but the spacecraft was behind schedule as well.

The later model of the AGC added a divide and a subtract instruction. The AGC was critical for guidance and navigation. The computer was a 16-bit, 1's complement machine, with a 1.7 microsecond, 12-step cycle time (current machines are sub-nano-second). It had 2048 bytes of random access memory, and 36k of read-only memory, both implemented in a magnetic core technology. The software was released in January of 1966, with the first flight was in August 1966. The design was used until 1975. No in-flight errors were ever attributed to software. None. This was after 2,000 person-years of independent verification and validation (IV&V).

The read-only memory, also implemented in magnetic core technology, was referred to as "core ropes." Here, the default was storing a "1", and if a "0" was desired, a wire was not passed through the core. They were linear structures, not 2- or 3- dimensional. When the coders had done their job, a map of 1's and 0's was passed on to Raytheon, who manufactured the core ropes, which generally changed with each mission. Only ladies well practiced in knitting had the patience to hand-manufacturer these. Our dominance in the space race with the Russians depended on the dexterity and exact threading of US needle workers.

The later model AGC had 11 instructions, including a double precision multiply. The unit included 20 counters, 60 discrete inputs, 18 discrete outputs, and 5 interrupts.

Parity calculations were applied to items stored in memory.

The software for the AGC contained an Executive program, that arranged the order of execution for up to 7 independent program modules. A priority scheduling scheme was implemented by a program called Waitlist. In lieu of a modern real-time operating system, the Executive scheduled tasks in priority order. It could handle 8 tasks, one executing, and 7 waiting. In 1968, there were about 400 programmers working on the AGC code.

Telemetry from the AGC used a single telemetry channel operating at 64 Khz. In this system, a Group was 1 second of data, 64k bits. A Frame was 20 mSec of pulses, or 1280 bits. A group contained 50 frames. A telemetry word was 8 bits, and 160 words fit in a frame.

The AGC had an associated display and keyboard unit for human interaction. This was called the Display and keyboard Assembly (DSKY). The keyboard had 16 keys. The display was electroluminescent, seven-segment format, and displayed 18 decimal digits and 3 signs. In actual use, an Apollo mission would require more than ten thousand keystrokes by an Astronaut.

The power supply for the AGC supplied 13 volts at 2.5 amps and two 3-volt lines at 3 amps and 22 amps. The AGC could be placed in a reduced power, stand-by mode.

The AGC had failure-detection built in. An alarm light was activated by a fault, and the machine continued to run. The overhead cost of the error checking circuitry was estimated to be 5%. Errors could be caused by a failed parity check, clock failure, a trap instruction, a timer on the interrupted state, and a power failure.

There were two Apollo Guidance computers per mission, one in the Command Module; and one in the Lunar Lander. This proved to be a good idea on Apollo 13, which suffered an explosion that crippled the Command module power system on the way to the moon. The computer in the Lunar Lander was re-tasked to provide guidance computations to get the astronauts back to Earth, before the Command Module would be re-activated for re-entry.

The guidance computers had 152 kilobytes of storage for the entire mission. The size was 6 inches, x 1 foot x 2 feet; they weighed 70 pounds, and used 55 watts of electricity. They were constructed of 5600 3-input nor gates, and featured a cycle time 11.7 microseconds.

The computer had a complexity of some 5,000 RTL logic gates from Fairchild Semiconductor (a pc has 100's of millions), which represented some 60% of the total US production of microcircuits at the time. The computer was a 16-bit machine, and had a 1.7 microsecond cycle time (current machines are sub-nano-second). It had 2048 bytes of random access memory, and 36k of read-only memory, both implemented in a magnetic core technology. There were four registers, the accumulator, the program counter, the remainder from the DIV instruction or the return address after a transfer of control instruction, and the lower product after a multiply instruction. There were five vectored interrupts. The clock was 1.024 MHz.

MIT's instrumentation lab had an early IBM model 650 mainframe, and rented time on 704's, 709's, and 7090's when needed. The IBM 650 was replaced by a Honeywell H-800. This was a 48-bit machine produced in conjunction with Raytheon. An instruction included an opcode and 3 operands per word. Four banks of core memory, each 2048 words, could be added. It had up to 4 magnetic tape drives, a printer, and a card reader-punch. It's assembly language was called Argus, Automatic Routine Generating and Updating System. It could run the Fortran language. The machine could barely keep up with the increasing demands, and was upgraded to an model 1800 by 1964. Up to 12 more memory banks could be added, and 8 megabytes of disk secondary storage.

A hybrid simulation machine based on Beckman analog computers and a SDS-9300 digital computer were used for Command module and lunar module cockpit simulations.

Although the Saturn Booster used its own guidance system, the AGC monitored launch parameters and provided indications that the launch was on course. The program was started automatically or by astronaut input.

The AGC interfaced with the Inertial Reference Platform in the Command Module, and with the astronauts, via a keypad and numeric display.

The calculations were done internally in metric, but the astronauts (mostly test pilots) preferred English units for display. (What's the worst that could happen?)

An HP-65 handheld scientific calculator was carried on the later Apollo-Soyuz mission, circa 1975, to perform calculations for the rendezvous maneuvers. This was a backup to the Apollo computer onboard the craft. By that time, the complexity of the HP-65 exceeded that of the AGC.

Service Module

The Service Module was located behind the Command Module, and the astronauts had no direct access to it. It was unpressurized, and contained a restartable liquid rocket engine and associated propellant, fuel cells, and electronics to support the mission. The fuel cells used hydrogen and oxygen, and some oxygen was also used to replenish the Command Module atmosphere. It had a reaction control system to adjust the spacecraft attitude. The service module had radiators to dump excess heat, and a high gain antenna to communicate with Earth. The

Command Module stayed attached to the Service Module until just before reentry into the atmosphere, when the Service module was commanded to reenter the atmosphere independently and burn. The Service Module relied on the AGC in the Command Module for computation.

The hard calculations were done on the ground, on big mainframes, based on radar data. Precomputed values were then uplinked to the Guidance Computer in the Command Module. The Guidance Computer was a key component of the Primary Guidance, Navigation and Control System (PGNCS) which also included the inertial subsystem and the optics subsystem. The uploaded data specified the position, velocity, and orientation of the spacecraft, an entity called the state vector. The crew could then update the onboard version of the state vector with navigation settings – the observations of fixed stars. These state vectors would be compared, and corrections made. A complete set of state vectors would include three parameters for position, and three for velocity. State vectors were valid for a particular time, and with respect to a particular frame of reference, which could be the fixed stars, the Earth, the Moon, or the Sun. The AGC values were updated on the launch pad, before launch, and during flight.

The AGC included a self-test routine. The AGC did its calculations in English units, altitude in nautical miles, velocity in feet per second (per the preference of the Astronauts, who were primarily test pilots). The position of the moon with respect to the Earth was specified in an Ephemeris of 6 elements, plus time. The difference between the measured values and the calculated values resulted in a correction, to be applied by the thrusters. The value of the Ephemeris was represented in the computer as a set of 9th order Taylor Series co-efficients. This was an approximation to the actual values, representable in double precision values in the AGC. Internally, the AGC represented distance in meters, and time in centi-seconds.

The Inertial System (gyros) and the optics subsystem interfaced with the computer via the Coupling Data Units (CDU's). These units functioned as analog to digital converters, and also digital to analog converters for computed values to command the IMU gimbals.. The computer difference between the (ground) observed vector and the onboard observed vector could be adjusted and minimized by thruster firings.

The IMU was the stable platform of reference for the spacecraft, with respect to the fixed stars. It included rate-integrating gyros and accelerometers. The IMU could be re-referenced during flight by a manual procedure. All gyros exhibit drift, which introduces a growing error between the sensed position, and the actual position. This grows with time, until the gyros need to be re-referenced.

The Optics subsystem had a sextant and a scanning telescope. It used the stars as fixed points of reference.

The User Interface of the Apollo Guidance Computer was the Display and Keyboard Assembly (DSKY) . There were two DSKY units in different locations in the module. To accommodate the wishes of the Astronauts, the interface with the DSKY was in the form of verbs and nouns. Verbs signified actions, and nouns, data items. There were 40 different verbs.

The inertial attitude (attitude with respect to the fixed stars) could be displayed, as well as the attitude with respect to Earth, or the Moon.

The Stabilization and Control System (SCS) included a series of thrusters to adjust the spacecraft's attitude, based on computer-derived or manual entry commands.

LEM

The lunar excursion module allowed a two man crew to land on the lunar surface, stay for a period of exploration, and return to the Apollo Command and Service Modules in lunar orbit. It had an Apollo Guidance Computer, programmed for the different and difficult tasks of landing on the lunar surface, and later taking off from the surface. Compared to the Launch complex at KSC with all its support infrastructure, the computer in the LEM did not have a lot to work with. The ability of the Command Module and LEM to do in-flight computations was crucial to this approach. At the time, the only guidance computers were developed for ballistic missiles.

The Lunar Module also had a separate Abort Guidance System Computer (AGSC). If the primary guidance system (which included the AGC) failed, the AGSC could be used to return the LEM to a safe lunar orbit, and await rendezvous by the Command Module. It was not capable of accomplishing a lunar landing. It was custom-built by TRW. The computer was called the MARCO 4418, MARCO referring to "MAn Rated COmputer". It weighed about 32 pounds, and used 90 watts of power. The memory was 18-bit serial access. There was 4096 words of memory, the lower half being RAM, and the upper half being ROM. Integer data types were 2's complement, and addresses were 13 bits. The machine had several registers, including an accumulator and an Index Register. There were 27 different instructions, and the software was written in assembly language. This was a real-time control computer, operating different tasks on a major cycle of 2 seconds, with minor cycles of 20 or 40 milliseconds. It was never required, but was used as a backup on Apollo 11.

Tasks for the main Apollo Guidance System (AGS) included radar data processing, calculation of orbital parameters, computation of rendezvous sequence, calibration of IMU sensors, engine commands, external signal sampling, attitude control, IMU signal processing, update of PGNCS downlink data, and update of direction cosines. The AGS was used three times, all successfully, including the Apollo-13 incident. Because of its lower power draw, and lower heat dissipation, the AGC calculated the burn for the return trip, as well as for two mid-course corrections.

There was a user interface panel, the data entry and display unit. Included a 9-digit read-out, and 16 push buttons, in a panel on the right side of the LEM, in front of the pilot.

The LEM had two sections, one of which held the descent engine, and stayed behind on the Lunar Surface. The Ascent Stage, holding the two astronauts and the Guidance Computer, rendezvoused with the Command and Service module in lunar orbit.

At Earth launch, the Lunar Module was located between the third stage of the Saturn-V vehicle, and the command module, in the Lunar Module adapter. The command module/capsule was detached, and turned around to dock with the lunar module. When that was latched in place, the assembly was turned back to an intercept orbit to the moon, and the command module's main engine was fired. It would fire again to achieve a lunar orbit, to depart the lunar orbit after the surface exploration, and to enable reaching Earth orbit.

Launch Support

This section discusses the launch support computers at KSC.

VAB

The Saturn moon rockets were assembled at the Cape vertically in the Vehicle Assembly Building (VAB), on the Crawler-transporter, and checked out for flight. Before being erected on the crawler, each stage was inspected and tested after delivery. The stages had been checked out individually before shipment to the launch site. In the first three Saturn V flights, 40 serious defects were found and corrected at this point. .

As aerospace vehicles became more complex, so did their testing. This was addressed with the introduction of automated checkout computers. The checkout computers ran a test script to verify the functionality and safety of the missile systems. The Apollo spacecraft had 2500 test points, with 5000 on the Saturn launch vehicle. Automated test allowed a faster and more efficient test sequence, slicing weeks and months from the schedule. Data were archived in computer files on tape for later review. When a problem was detected, the test software would assist in a troubleshooting scenario.

The test computers were programmed in a language expressly designed for use in testing, by test engineers. This was different from the operational software. Early efforts at Marshall Space Flight Center focused on these languages. Each of the major component manufacturers had their own test computers and languages, generally referred to as system test oriented languages (STOL).

A test engineer was compelled to learn a programming language, or to relay on expressing his or her wishes to a programmer, who saw the test language as rather primitive. One such language was the circa-1963 ATOLL, Acceptance Test or Launch Language. Integrated vehicle testing took place in the VAB, and was about 90% automated.

The VAB was built to integrate and test the Saturn-V rocket and the Apollo payload. It is the largest single story building in the world at over 500 feet tall, needing all that headroom to hold the erected Saturn moon rocket. It was completed in 1966, and was later used for assembly of the Space Shuttle missions.

Launch Complex 39

Launch Complex 39 at KSC was used to launch the Lunar Missions. It has two launch pads, 39a and 39B, and included the Vertical Assembly Building and the connecting crawler way. These were later used for the Space Shuttle Program.

The Mobile Launch Platform

The Mobile Launcher Platform, or crawler, carried the assembled Saturn-V rocket and Apollo payload from the Vertical Assembly Building 3 miles to the launch pad. The vehicle also included a Launch Umbilical Tower, a crane, and the water suppression system, which protected the assembly at launch. The platform on the crawler adjusted automatically to keep the vehicle vertical during the trip to the launch pad, which was on a 3% grade. The crawler was built by the Marion Power Shovel Company, of Marion, Ohio, and later used for the Space Shuttle. It had a RCA-110 Computer Mainframe that could talk to the Control Rooms, when it was not in motion.

The Launch Control Center

The Launch Control Center at Kennedy Space Center had control of the Apollo launch until the vehicle cleared the launch tower, at which point control transferred to Mission Control in Houston. The LCC is Building 30 at KSC, located near the Vertical Assembly Building. It has two facilities called the Mission Operations Control Rooms. One is on the second floor, and the other is on the third floor. Room number 2, used for the Apollo Missions, including the Lunar Landings, was designated a National Historic Landmark and has been restored back to its configuration at that time.

When the various stages of the Saturn-V vehicle were assembled in the VAB, the rocket was connected to the Launch Control Center for checkout, via a high speed data line. After checkout, the crawler-transporter picked up the vehicle and its support base, and moved it to the launchpad. Here, the vehicle was connected to data lines leading from the pad to the LCC again.

Both in the VAB and at the pad, RCA computers in the LCC controlled the automated testing and verification. Tests are conducted from one of the firing rooms in the LCC.

For checkout operations, a firing room would be occupied by up to 400 engineers, with additional support personnel in a backup room. There were 400 consoles, 100 of which were CRT displays. There was also four large overhead screens with projectors.

Checkout and Launch Control Computers

The circa-1961 RCA-110 Computer Mainframe served as the checkout and launch control computer for the Saturn Vehicle. One was located in each of the four firing rooms in the Launch control Complex. There was another underground at each launch pad, and one on each of the Mobile Launch Platforms. The test software was developed at the Astrionics Lab at MSFC with support from the launch support team in Florida. The RCA-110A models had increased memory over the earlier 110 model. The computer automated the entire preflight checkout process. The master computer in the blockhouse and the slave computer at the launch pad were connected by a coaxial cable. The launch pad computer interfaced with the vehicle computer in the IU through an umbilical.

The RCA-110 was also the basis for the automated checkout equipment for the S-1C stage, and the IU. The computer manuals can be found here:

TP1134_RCA110_PrgmRef_Aug62.pdf.

http://bitsavers.trailing-edge.com/pdf/rca/110/

The RCA-110 was a 24-bit fixed-point process control machine. It was implemented in solid-state electronics, with a clock speed of 936 KHz, and had 72 instructions. It supported four levels of priority interrupts, and had accumulators and index registers. There were also eight Input-Output registers. The add or subtract operation took 57 microseconds, a multiply took 728 microseconds, and a divide, 868 microseconds.

Memory consisted of 256 to 4096 words of core memory, later expanded. Secondary storage was provided by a magnetic drum assembly, rotating at 3,600 rpm, and providing 8.3 millisecond access to data. The drum held up to 51,200 words. Data were transferred to the computer at a 200 kilohertz rate. The computer unit was 82" x 34" x 105" in size, and required 5,000 watts of power at 220 volts. IBM wrote the "Saturn operating system" for the RCA computers, and the test software.

NASA established a large computer center at Slidell, Mississippi to serve both the Mississippi Test Facility (MTF), and the Michoud operations. This had been originally built as a large mainframe computer center for the FAA. Michoud was the production facility for the large Saturn-V first stage, and the MTF was where the stage's engines were test fired.

In the firing rooms, a DDP-224 minicomputer was used to drive the video displays. This was a 24-bit core memory machine built by the Computer Control Company of Massachusetts. This company later became part of Honeywell. The computer manual can be found here:

http://bitsavers.org/pdf/honeywell/ddp-24/DDP-24_InstructionMan_Aug64.pdf

Mission Control Center (MCC) at JSC

Control and authority over the mission of the Mission transitioned from KSC to JSC Mission Control when the vehicle cleared the launch tower, which took about 12 seconds.

The Control Center was used for the shuttle flights, and is still used for Space Station operations. It has been renamed the Christopher C. Kraft Mission Control Center. It consists of one large operational control center that operates 24x7, with resources for the various flight controllers. Because of the possibility of hurricanes in the Houston-Gulf area, there are backup sites at MSFC in Huntsville, and GSFC in Maryland. The original Control Center developed for the Apollo Lunar landings was driven by a large IBM Mainframe Computer (System S/360). A similar configuration was used at Goddard and Marshall. These facilities were up and operational during any Mission, and could handover control quickly. NASCOM, the NASA worldwide communication network was located at Goddard Space Flight Center, and connected to the world-side network of tracking stations and tracking ships. All the data flowed into the basement of Building 14 at Goddard, and was sent to the various NASA Centers as required. A direct line from the launch site in Florida to the Marshall Space Flight Center in Alabama was maintained.

The Real Time computer complex at Mission Control (Building 30) at JSC was based on five IBM mainframes of the System/360 family. The previous Gemini Missions had been supported by up to five of the IBM 7094-II computers. Gemini involved the simultaneous operation of two spacecraft in orbit (for rendezvous), and introduced video graphics displays. Mission control for Mercury and early Gemini had been done at the Kennedy Launch Center. The Control Center in Houston got the first S/360 shipped by IBM. The operating system OS/360 was not well suited to real time operations, being designed for batch processing. IBM introduced a real-time version, RTOS/360, with better real time response. Five NASA S/360 model 75's were used at JSC.

from, http://www-03.ibm.com/ibm/history/exhibits/mainframe/mainframe_PP2075.html.

"The Model 75 was an outgrowth of IBM's continuing engineering development effort to enhance the capabilities of the original System/360 offerings. Its main memory operated at 750 nanoseconds and was available in three sizes up to 1,048,576 characters of information. The memory was interleaved up to four ways to obtain increased performance.

The Model 75 superseded the original Model 70 of the System/360 family, which had been announced a year earlier. Manufactured at IBM's plant in Kingston, N.Y., the Model 75 had a monthly rental range of $50,000 to

$80,000, and a purchase price range of $2.2 million to $3.5 million. Deliveries began during the fourth quarter of 1965."

The S/360 series used punch card input, and large line printers for output. They used the IBM channel architecture for I/O, including disk and 9-track tape drives.

The Model 75 was near the top of the System/360 family in terms of size and performance. In the System/360, an 8-bit byte was standardized, and memory was byte addressable. Words were 32-bits in size, in big-endian format. CPU's were microcoded, and floating point operations were supported. Twenty-four bit addressing was supported, as were prioritized interrupts, crucial for real-time operation.

Generally, only one computer would be on-line during a mission, with one more in backup mode. Every hour, the online system was backed up to tape, so a complete transition could be made in the case of failure. During launch and critical operations, two machines were kept online. There were five units, so two Apollo missions or simulations could be supported simultaneously.

The Command, Communication, and Telemetry System (CCATS) handled input/output, and used three Univac 494 computers. These were 30-bit machines with 131K to 262K of core memory. Up to 24 I/O channels were available and the system was usually shipped with UNIVAC magnetic drum storage. The basic operating system was OMEGA. For real time commanding, at the commanding uplink station, a Univac 124B was used.

The 494 was a 30 bit machine with 131k or core memory, and 24 I/O channels. It used magnetic drum storage. It came with the OMEGA operating system. The 1230 was also a 30-bit machine,

Apollo tracking sites around the world used Univac 1230 machines, replacing the earlier 1218's used for Gemini support. These talked to Univac 494's at NASCOM, Goddard Space Flight Center, Building 14. This, in turn, was linked to JSC over 40.8 KBPS lines. A 1218 also drove the big screen display in Mission Control.

A Univac 481, from MCC at Houston, is at the American Computer & Robotics Museum in Bozeman, Montana, if you're in the neighborhood.

Reference:

http://arstechnica.com/information-technology/2014/04/50-years-ago-ibm-created-mainframe-that-helped-bring-men-to-the-moon/

It is interesting to note that the IBM S/360 architecture was the basis for the 5 computers onboard the Space Shuttle, the AP-101's.

The Apollo missions required extensive ground tracking and data acquisition support. To meet these requirements, the Manned Space Flight Tracking Network along with certain elements of the Department of Defense Gulf and Eastern Test Ranges supported the missions through initial Earth orbits, after which the Goddard Space Flight Center's STADAN (Space Tracking and Data Acquisition Network) assumed responsibility for monitoring and tracking the spacecraft. Goddard was the location of the Network Operations Control Center (NOCC) in the basement of Building 14. Stadan's coverage was limited, however, to about 15 minutes of every 90 minute Earth Orbit. To provide more coverage for the manned missions, the Manned Space Flight Network (MSFN) was established. Some of the tracking sites were actually ships, to provide coverage over areas where there was no convenient land. In addition to these, there are three big antennas positioned roughly equally around the World (California, Australia, and Spain) that formed the Deep Space Network. The Tracking and Data Relay Satellites at Geosynchronous orbit came later, in 2009.

During the Apollo Program, the system of data tracking systems was called the Apollo Network. These stations provided range/range-rate data, and communications in both directions. The JPL Systems of S-band (2-4 GHz) transceivers and antennas was used.

The GSFC was the operational nerve center of NASA's worldwide voice and data communications network, and provided tracking and telemetry data from the various ground stations to the other NASA Centers.

Goddard's MSFN real-time computing system determined orbital insertion conditions and provided the network with acquisition information during early phase of the mission. During the reentry period the real-time system was used for predictions and impact determination.

To cover gaps in the coverage due to the oceans, NASA used a series of ships, each configured as a ground station. These were the USNS Vanguard, Redstone, and Mercury. The ships were modified by removing the bow and stern of a tanker, and adding a new mid section for the electronics and crew. They were 595 feet long with a beam of 75 feet. Fully loaded, they displaced over 23,000 tons. They could achieve 17 knots, but tracking was usually done at 13 knots. They had an endurance capability of over 20,000 nautical miles.

These ships carried a full Mission Control Center, including a Command Communicator, four Vehicle Monitors (Flight Controllers) , an aeromedical monitor, and Flight Dynamics Monitor. This was a backup to the control center at Goddard, which was the backup to Houston.

The complement of computers onboard included Sperry-Univac 624B's and Univac 1218's. The 1218 was a militarized 418, in a cabinet 6 feet tall and weighing 775 pounds. It used 18-bit core memory, and could be configured with 4k to 64k of memory. In Navy use, it was a fire control computer, circa 1963.

The Skylab Missions

By the time that the Saturn rocket had put men on the moon and returned them safely multiple times, the Apollo computers were mostly obsolete. This was due to major advances in hardware and software, largely driven by the Apollo effort. Using spare Saturn-V's, the next project was the Skylab space station. This used a Saturn IVB stage as the structure for the station, launched by a Saturn-V with live first and second stages. Astronauts were carried to the facility in-orbit on three missions in 1973-1974 by Apollo capsules on Saturn-Ib vehicles. Skylab was in orbit until 1979, when it reentered the atmosphere.

With a large volume of science data to be managed, the AGC was not up to the job. The IBM System/4Pi TC-1, a derivative of the IBM S/360 mainframe, and a relative of the subsequent Shuttle's AP-101, was used. This was a radiation-hardened unit, with a 16-bit word, and 16k of memory. It had a custom-designed input-output unit for the lab. It drew 56 watts of electrical power, and weighed 18 pounds. It was built with ttl-technology integrated circuits, and core memory. Ten were built, and two were flown. A standard S/360 mainframe was used to produce code for the 4Pi, and a simulator was used for verification. A System/360-75 was used to evaluate the onboard computer's performance in orbit. It could run a simulation at 3.5 times less than real-time. There was also a hybrid simulator, with a System/360 model 44 hooked to a 4Pi.

The 4Pi had 54 different instruction, and supported 32-bit double precision data. Cycle time was 3 microseconds. An add took 3 cycles, and a multiply or divide took 16. It had a 24-bit real-time clock. A simple numeric keyboard was used to communicate with the computer in the lab in orbit, and it could also be loaded via uplink, and by an onboard tape drive.

The first Skylab mission lasted 272 days, followed by an unmanned period of 394 days, when the computer kept things going. The computer was turned off for 4 years while NASA discussed reboosting Skylab to a higher orbit, or letting it reenter. There was a need to put some mods in the software, but the tools and card decks containing the code had been discarded. This resulted in some 2500 cards being re-punched from listings. At the end of 4 years, the onboard computer was booted up by ground command, and the updates worked fine.

Manufacturer's Sites

The Apollo rocket was built by many manufacturers across the United States. These manufacturers used state-of-the art mainframe computers to support the massive calculations needed. In that time frame, late 1950's through 1970, the mainframe market was dominated by

"IBM and the Seven Dwarfs." These were UNIVAC, NCR, Control Data, Honeywell, General Electric, RCA, and Burroughs. Most of the machines were 32 bit, but Univac stuck with 36 bit words. The IBM dominance was due to their development of the System/360 series, from the legacy of their 704/7040 and 709/7090 machines. The follow-on mainframe to the S/360 architecture is still being produced.

Mainframe I/O was offloaded in the IBM architecture to Communication channels, essentially, a computer who job it was to interface with storage and devices and printers. The Channel offloaded these asynchronous tasks from the main computer part, allowing it to function more efficiently on big calculations. Peripherals of the period included card readers, line printers, magnetic tape drives, data storage drums, and later, disks. Memory in the units was predominately magnetic core. The circuitry was transistor based, a big improvement on the previous generation's vacuum tubes. Integrated circuits would come later.

Mainframes typically occupied a large room, heavily air conditioned, and with a raised floor for running interconnect cables between units.

The usage scenario was that you produced a deck of punched cards, and submitted it for a run on the computer. When your turn came, the operator fed in your cards, and the computer was exclusively yours until run to completion. At the end of the run, you got your cards and a print-out back. With luck, you could access the computer on a daily basis.

For automated factory test of Apollo assemblies, NASA specified a CDC-924A machine This was programmed in a special test language, ATOLL – Acceptance, Test or Launch Language.

Chrysler Aerospace was a branch of automobile marker Chrysler Corporation. Chrysler's Central Engineering Office was a national resource, used by the Army Signal Corps to manufacture radar antennas during World War-II. In 1950, Chrysler became the support contractor to the Army's Ordnance Guided Missile Center at the Redstone Arsenal in Huntsville, Alabama. This facility was where von Braun and the German Rocket Team had been sent. Chrysler set up a Missile Division to produce the Redstone Missile that the team had designed. Chrysler, working with von Braun, designed and produced the follow-on Jupiter missile. The Redstone missile was the launch vehicle for the Mercury suborbital manned missions. Chrysler became the prime contractor for the first stage of the Saturn I and Saturn IB vehicles. Chrysler built the S-1 booster for the Apollo program in the Michoud Assembly Facility near New Orleans. Werner von Braun's brother Magnus worked at Chrysler in the Missile Division in 1955, transferring later to the Car Division, and later serving as the UK export director.

North American Aviation built the Apollo Command and Service Modules, and the second stage (S-II) of the

Saturn-V rocket. They also built the Little Joe boosters that were used to test the launch escape system of the Mercury and Apollo capsules. The S-II stage was subjected to automated test by a CDC-924A transistor-based mainframe computer. This was a 24-bit version of the 48-bit CDC 1604. They used magnetic core memory for storage. The CDC machines were designed by Seymour Cray. The 1600 series was used as the guidance computer (ground-based) for the Minuteman missile. You can see a CDC-924 in the first Terminator movie, where it runs the machinery in a factory. The manuals for the CDC-924 computer can be found here:

http://bitsavers.informatik.uni-stuttgart.de/pdf/cdc/924/

Grumman Aircraft Company at Bethpage, Long Island, New York, built 13 of the Apollo Lunar Modules as chief contractor to NASA. Grumman had built a series of important naval aircraft during World War-II. They changed their name to Grumman Aerospace in 1969 to indicate their new focus. They competed, unsuccessfully, for the Space Shuttle contract. They also produced a series of early observation spacecraft, including the Orbiting Astronautical Observatory (OAO).

Boeing built the S-1C stage at the Michoud Assembly Facility, near New Orleans, starting in 1961. This facility had deep water access, and the massive stage was transported by barge to the Kennedy Space Center. At Slidell, Louisiana, about 12 miles from Michoud, NASA built what was at the time one of the largest computer centers in the country, with both analog and digital computers.

Douglas Aircraft Company in California built the S-IVB stage. This stage was small enough to be transported by air, using NASA's "Pregnant Guppy" aircraft. Automated checkout of the stage was implemented by a CDC-924A mainframe. Before the computer was used, the checkout could take 1200 hours. It was reduced to 500, and with additional testing included.

IBM Corporation in Huntsville, near MSFC, built the the Instrument Unit. It had been developed at MSFC's Astrionics Laboratory, and was transitioned over to IBM to build. The subcontractor for the intricate cooling system of the IU was International Harvester's Solar Division.

Lockheed Propulsion Company, a Division of Lockheed Aircraft, built the Launch Escape System that sat atop the Apollo Capsule.

General Motors, AC Spark Plug Division produced the inertial measurement units (IMU's).

Raytheon Corporation built the AGC's under contract to MIT's Instrumentation Labs.

How did it all work out? Apollo-11 landed successfully on the moon, and the astronauts were able to return safely to Earth. There were some moments of panic, as the lander computer became overloaded and issued alarms. But the hardware and software were operating as designed, giving resources to critical tasks, and ignoring tasks that could wait. Actually, this condition was caused by a manual error – the rendezvous radar had been left in the wrong mode.

AGC's supported the early Earth orbiting missions, the six lunar landing missions, the three Skylab missions, and the Apollo-Soyuz mission. An AGC was later flown on an F-8 research plane in a fly-by-wire test.

Apollo 12 was struck by lightning after liftoff. Power was lost momentarily to the computer and guidance system. But everything was reset and checked out in Earth orbit, and the mission continued.

Apollo 13 certainly showed the flexibility of the AGC. The astronauts had to retreat to the Lunar Module, when an explosion in the service module knocked out the fuel cells on the way to the moon. The command module and its engine was critical to returning to Earth, and a safe reentry. The Lunar Module's AGC was re-purposed to calculate the proper attitude and duration of the burns, and the crew returned safely. It made for a great movie.

By the time Apollo flew, many computers were faster and better than the AGC, but the AGC got the job done, and kicked off an entire industry of real time control computers that remains a growth sector to this day. Yes, your cell phone has more processing power.

Would you trust your life to it, to get you to the moon and back? Good luck with that.

Afterword

Most of the Apollo support facility's have been repurposed to the follow-on Artemis Program. This includes the Vertical Assembly Building, the Crawler-Transporters, and the launch pad facility's.

The launch of Artemis is imminent as I write this.

Glossary

ABMA – Army Ballistic Missile Agency, Redstone Arsenal, Huntsville, Alabama.

AGC – Apollo Guidance Computer.

AGS – Apollo Guidance System.

AGSC – Abort Guidance System Computer.

AIAA – American Institute of Aeronautics and Astronautics.

ALU – arithmetic logic unit

AMD – Aircraft Missiles Division, Fairchild Hiller, Hagerstown, MD.

AOMC – Army Ordnance Missile Command – 1958, Redstone Arsenal, JPL, WSPG.

Apogee – farthest point in the orbit from the Earth.

ARPA – Advanced Research projects Agency.

ASC –Advanced Spacecraft Computer, by IBM, for Titan launch vehicle.

ASIN – Amazon Standard Book Number.

Astrionics – electronics for space flight.

ATOLL - Acceptance Test or Launch Language

BP – boilerplate. Mechanical model.

CDC – Control Data Corporation.

CDU – coupling data unit (IMU and optics interface with AGC).

Cpu – central processing unit

Cyrogenic – pertaining to very low temperatures.

DoD – Department of Defense.

DSKY – Apollo guidance computer' display and keyboard assembly.

DSN – Deep Space Network.

DTM – dynamic test model, for structural tests.

Ephemeris – position information data set for orbiting bodies, 6 parameters plus time.

FAA – Federal Aviation Administration

Gimbal – pivoted support, allowing rotation about 1 axis.

Gpm – gallons per minute.

GSFC – NASA Goddard Space Flight Center, Greenbelt, MD.

Gyro – device to measure angular rate.

H1 – Rocketdyne engine, used on Saturn-I first stage.

IBSN - International Standard Book Number

ICBM – Intercontinental Ballistic Missile.

IBM – International Business Machines Company.

IMU – inertial measurement unit

Interrupt – signaling mechanism for input/output devices on a computer.

IRBM – Intermediate Range Ballistic Missile.

ISP – specific impulse. Measure of efficiency of rocket engine. Units of seconds.

IU – Instrument Unit.

JPL – Jet Propulsion Laboratory, Pasadena, CA.

JSC – Johnson Space Center, Houston, Texas.

Jupiter – ICBM, 3-stage. Developed by von Braun Team.

Kbps – kilo (103) bits per second.

Khz – kilohertz, one thousand cycles per second.

Kev – kilo electron volts, measure of energy of a particle.

KSC – NASA Kennedy Space Center, launch site, Florida.

Lbf – pounds, force.

LC-37 – Launch Complex – 37 at KSC.

LEM – lunar excursion module.

LEO – low Earth orbit.

LES – Apollo Launch Escape System.

LH2 – liquid hydrogen.

LOX – liquid oxygen, boils at -297 F.

LVDA – Launch Vehicle Data Adapter.

LVDC – Launch Vehicle Digital Computer.

MCC – Mission control Center, at JSC.

Mev – million electron volts, measure of energy of a
    particle.

MINITRACK – "Minimum Trackable Satellite " U. S.
    satellite tracking network, 1957.

MIT – Massachusetts Institute of Technology

MMC – Micrometeoroid Measurement Capsule, original
name of Pegasus.

MSC – Manned Space Center, Houston, TX. Renamed
    JSC.

MSFC – NASA Marshall Space Flight Center,
    Huntsville, AL.

MSFN – Manned Space Flight Network.

m/s – meters per second.

MTF – (NASA) Mississippi Test Facility.

NASA – National Aeronautics and Space Administration.

NASCOM – NASA Communications Network.
Worldwide, operated by GSFC.

NCR – National Cash Register (computer manufacturer)

NOCC – Network Operations Control Center (GSFC).

Nor – negative "or" logic

NORAD – North American Air Defense.

NRL – Naval Research Lab, Washington, DC.

NTIS – National Technical Information Service
    (www.ntis.gov).

PAM – pulse amplitude modulation.

Pc – personal computer

PCM – pulse code modulation.

Perigee – closest point in the orbit from the Earth.

PGNCS – Primary Guidance, Navigation, and Control system for Apollo.

POGO – longitudinal oscillation in liquid-fueled rocket motors that can lead to failure.

Pregnant Guppy – large cargo aircraft operated by Aero Spacelines 1963-1979.

RAM – Random Access Memory – generally, read-write.

ROM – Read-Only Memory, used for storage of instructions and fixed data.

R&D – research & development.

RCA – Radio Corporation of America (computer manufacturer).

Redstone – Army missile developed by the von Braun team. Used for Mercury manned flights.

Redstone Arsenal – Army R&D facility in Huntsville, AL. Later became NASA MSFC

RP-1 – rocket propellant-one, highly refined kerosene.

RTL – resistor-transistor logic

SA – x – Saturn-Apollo – flight x.

SAO – Smithsonian Astrophysical Observatory.

SI – System International – the metric system.

S-IC – first stage of the Saturn V

S-II – second stage of the Saturn V

S-IVB – third stage of the Saturn V

S-IV – second stage of Saturn 1 rocket.

STADAN – Space Tracking and Data Acquisition Network.

STOL – System Test Oriented Language.

TDRS – Tracking and Data Relay Satellite

Titan – ICBM and NASA/USAF launch vehicle.

TM – Technical Manual.

TTL – transistor-transistor logic

Ullage – residual fuel or oxidizer in a tank after engine burn is complete.

V-2 – German World War-II missile developed by the von Braun Team.

Vdc – volts, direct current.

WSMR – White Sands Missile Range, New Mexico.

References

Aldrin, Buzz No Dream Is Too High, Life Lessons From a Man Who Walked on the Moon, National Geographic, 2016, ISBN-9781426216497.

Bilstein, Roger E. Stages to Saturn: A Technological History of the Apollo/Saturn Launch Vehicles. 1980, NASA SP-4206. ISBN 0-16-048909-1.

Caudle, John M.; Colbert, Donald C. Flight Control computer for Saturn Space Vehicles, MSFC.

Ceruzzi, Paul E. Beyond the Limits, Flight Enters the Computer Age, 1989, MIT Press, ISBN 0-262-03143-4.

Decher, Rudolf The Astrionics System of Saturn Launch Vehicles, NASA TM X-53384, MSFC, Feb 1966.

Dickinson, M. M.; Jackson, J. B.; Randa, G. C.; IBM Space Guidance Center, Owego, NY, Saturn V Launch Vehicle Digital Computer and Data Adapter, Proceedings of the Fall Joint Computer Conference, 1964, pages 501-516.

Goodwin, Robert, Apollo Project, the Test Program, Apogee Books, ISBN 1-894959-36-1.

Haeusserman, Walter "Guidance and Control of Saturn Launch Vehicles," July, 1965, AIAA Paper 65-304, presented at AIAA Second Annual Meeting, San Francisco, CA.

Haeusserman, Walter Description and Performance of the Saturn Launch Vehicle's Navigation, Guidance, and Control, NASA/MSFC, July, 1970, NASA TN D-5869.

Hall, Eldon C. Journey to the Moon: The History of the Apollo Guidance Computer, 1996, AIAA Press, ISBN 1-56347-185-X.
Hopkins, Albert; Alonso, Ramon; Blair-Smith; Hugh; Logical Description for the Apollo Guidance Computer (AGC 4), MIT Instrumentation Laboratory, 1963, Report R-393.
IBM, Saturn 1b/V Instrument Unit Technical Manual, Instrumentation system Description, (updated for Sat V??)
IBM, Saturn V Launch Vehicle Digital Computer, NASA Part Number 50M35010, IBM Part Number 6109030, Volume 1, General Description and Theory, Nov. 30, 1964.
IBM, Technical Description of IBM System/4 Pi computers, 1967, https://archive.org/details/bitsavers_ibm4piTechBMSyste m4PiComputers1967_10147919
Lindsay, Hamish Tracking Apollo to the Moon, Springer, 2001, ISBN- 1852332123.
Low, George M., Apollo Spacecraft, NASA Manned Spacecraft Center, Houston, TX.
Lowery, H. R. Saturn Instrument Unit Command System, NASA TM X-53350, Oct. 1965.

Mindell, David A. Digital Apollo, 2011, MIT Press, ISBN 978-0-262-51610-5.

Moore, F. B.; White J. B. "Application of Redundancy in the Saturn V Guidance and Control System," NASA/MSFC, 67-553.

NASA The Apollo Flight Journal, The Apollo On-board Computers, http://history.nasa.gov/afj/compessay.htm

NASA/ John F. Kennedy Space Center, Saturn 1B and Saturn V Computer Programs, Software Status Report, July 5, 1972, NASA-TM-X-729C1, N76-13156, TR-612, Rev. 13
NASA/MSFC Astrionics System Handbook, Saturn Launch Vehicles, MSFC No. IV-4-401-1, IBM No. 68-966-0002, Nov. 1968.

NASA/MSFC SLCC ATOLL User's Manual, IBM 70-F11-0001, Huntsville, Ala. Dec 1970.

O'Brien, Frank The Apollo Guidance Computer: Architecture and Operation, Springer Praxis Books, 1st Edition, 2010, ISBN- 1441908765.

Orloff. Richard W. and Harland, David M. Apollo: The Definitive Sourcebook, Springer Praxis Books/Space Exploration, Springer; 1st ed., 200), ISBN-10: 0387300430.

Parker, Phil; The Apollo Flight Journal, The Apollo Onboard Computer, Spaceflight, J. British Interplanetary Society, Vol 16, No. 10, Cot 1974, pp 378-382.

http://history.nasa.gov/afj/compessay.htm

Powell, J. T. "Saturn Flight Instrumentation," Nov. 1964, ISA Journal, Vol. II, No. 11, PP 51-63.

RCA, RCA 110 Computer, Programmer's Reference Manual, August 1962, TP-1134

Stakem, Patrick H. The History of Spacecraft Computers from the V-2 to the Space Station, 2011, PRB Publishing, ASIN B004L626U6.

Stakem, Patrick H. The Saturn Rocket and the Pegasus Missions, 1965, 2012, PRRB Publishing, ASIN B00BVA79ZW.

Thomason, H. E. A General Description of the ST-124-M Inertial Platform System, NASA TN D-2983, Sept. 1965.

Tomayko, James E. Computers in Space, Journeys with NASA, 1994, alpha books, ISBN 1-56761-463-9.

Tomayko, James E. Computers in Spaceflight: The NASA Experience, 1988, NASA Technical Document 19880069935, Amazon digital Services, ASIN B001T4YUI4.

Early ballistic missile guidance

Bitzer, John A. Woerner, Ted A. A4-Fibel (English translation) Army Ballistic Missile Agency Redstone Arsenal, Al. 1957 ISBN 1-89-4643-14-3.

Dumont, Brian, "An Introduction to the Athena computer," May 16, 1969, Oregon State University.

Gray, George, "Some Burroughs Transistor Computers (including the Atlas Guidance computer)", Unisys History Newsletter, Volume 3, Number 1, March 1999.

Gray, George, "Sperry Rand Military Computers, 1957-1975," Unisys History Newsletter, Volume 3, Number 4, August 1999.
Apollo
Eyles, Don "Tales from the Lunar Module Guidance Computer," Feb. 6, 2004, AAS-04-064, 27th Annual Guidance and Control Conference.

Godwin, Robert Project Apollo: The Test Program, Volume 1, Collector's Guide Publishing, Inc. 2006, ISBN-1894959361.

Kraft, Jr. Christopher C. "Computers and the Space Program: An Overview," Jan. 1976, IBM J. Research & Development.

Logsdon, John M. John F. Kennedy and the Race to the Moon, Palgrave Macmillan, 2010, ISBN- 023011010X.

Martin, Frederick H. and Battin, Richard H. "Computer-Controlled Steering of the Apollo Spacecraft," J. Spacecraft, Vol 5, n 4, April 1968.

Orloff. Richard W. and Harland, David M. Apollo: The Definitive Sourcebook, Springer Praxis Books/Space Exploration, Springer; 1st ed., 200), ISBN-10: 0387300430.

Tracking Ships

Handbook for Apollo Instrumentation ships, avail, https://www.hq.nasa.gov/alsj/MG-402-Ships-Manual-OCR.pdf

Navy Recovery Ships, avail: https://history.nasa.gov/ships.html

Early spacecraft tracking ships, avail: http://www.collectspace.com/ubb/Forum29/HTML/0 00721-2.html

http://www.rangerat.com/

Orbital Mechanics

Logsdon, Tom Orbital Mechanics: Theory and Applications, 1997, Wiley-Interscience, ISBN 0471146366.

Prussing, John R and Conway, Bruce A. Orbital Mechanics, 1993, Oxford University Press, ISBN-0195078349.

V-2 and the von Braun team

21st Century Complete Guide to U.S. Army Redstone Arsenal History: Missiles, Rockets, von Braun, Space History (CD-ROM), 2002, Progressive Management; 1st ed, ISBN-1193182830X.

Dornberger, W. V-2, 1960, Ballantine, ASIN: B001O4M1MQ.

Dungan, T. D. V-2: A Combat History of the First Ballistic Missile, Westholme Publishing, 2005, ISBN-1594160120.

Huzel, Dieter. K. Peenemunde to Canaveral, 1962, Prentice-Hall Greenwood Press Reprint, May 12, 1981, ISBN-0313229287.

NASA, World Spaceflight News, Wernher von Braun: His Life and Work from German Missiles to the Saturn V Moon Rocket - An Expansive Compilation of Authoritative NASA History Documents and Selections, Progressive Management, 2012, ASIN: B007FFY48C.

Neufeld, Michael, von Braun, Dreamer of Space, Engineer of War, Vintage; Reprint edition, 2008, ISBN-0307389375.

Neufeld, Michael, The Rocket and the Reich, Peenemunde and the Coming of the Ballistic Missile Era, 1995, Smithsonian, 0-02-922895-6.

Nicaise, Placide D. Huntsville and the von Braun Rocket Team, 2003, ASIN B00AX2GL4E, 2003.

Ordway, Frederick I.; Sharp, Mitchell P. The Rocket Team 1979, Crowell, ISBN 0-690-01656-5.

Bergast, Erik Wernher von Braun, 1996, National Space Institute, ISBN 0-917680-01-4.

Hearing before the NASA Authorization Subcommittee of the Committee on Aeronautical and Space Sciences, United States Senate, Eighty-sixth Congress, second session, on H. J. Res. 567, a bill to effect immediately the transfer of the Development Operations Division of the Army Ballistic Missile Agency to the National Aeronautics and Space Administration, U.S. Govt. Printing Office, (1960), ASIN: B007HV5XX4.

von Braun, Wernher; Ordway, Frederick I., III; Durant, Fred Space Travel: A History: An Update of History of Rocketry & Space Travel, 1985, ISBN-0061818984.

Zaloga, Steven J. V-2 Ballistic Missile 1945-52, 2003, Osprey, ISBN 1841765414.

Redstone Missile

Bullard, John W. History of the Redstone Missile System, 1965, ASIN: B00ACXXQAQ.

Chrysler Corporation Missile Division, Army Ballistic Missile Agency, This is Redstone Missile Weapon System, Periscope Film LLC, 2012, ISBN- 1937684806.

Jupiter Missile

The Other Missiles of October: Eisenhower, Kennedy, and the Jupiters, 1957-1963, The University of North Carolina Press, October 1, 1997, ISBN- 0807846473.

Titan missile

Berhow, Mark U S Strategic and Defensive Missile Systems 1950-2004, Osprey Publishing, 2005, ISBN- 1841768383.

Launius, Roger D. (Ed) and Jenkins, Dennis R. (Ed) To Reach the High Frontier: A History of U.S. Launch Vehicles, The University Press of Kentucky; 1st ed, 2002, ISBN- 0813122457.

Van Riper, A.; Bowdoin Rockets and Missiles: The Life Story of a Technology, The Johns Hopkins University Press, 2007, ISBN- 0801887925.

http://www.hq.nasa.gov/alsj/LM17_Brief_History_Grumman_Aircraft_Corp_B5-6.pdf

Resources

American Institute of Aeronautics and Astronautics, www.aiaa.org

Apollo Guidance Computer emulator, http://www.ibiblio.org/apollo/index.html

Aviation Week and Space Technology, http://www.aviationweek.com/

Encyclopedia Astronautica, http://www.astronautix.com/

IBM Archives,
http://www-03.ibm.com/ibm/history/exhibits/space/space_saturn.html

NASA Technical Reports Server, http://ntrs.nasa.gov/

wikipedia, various.

The disposition of all Command Modules, and all unflown Service Modules is listed at http://en.wikipedia.org/wiki/Apollo_Command/Service_Module#CSMs_produced

All Service Modules flown were burned up in the Earth's atmosphere at termination of the missions.

All Instrument Units flown re-entered the atmosphere and burned. One unit is at the Smithsonian facility at Dulles Airport in Virginia, on display.

The disposition of all Lunar Modules is listed at: http://en.wikipedia.org/wiki/Apollo_Lunar_Module#Lunar_Modules_produced

http://nassp.sourceforge.net/wiki/PGNCS

Delco Electronics, Apollo 15, CM Software, General Motors Corp.

http://www.hq.nasa.gov/alsj/a15/A15Delco.pdf

http://history.nasa.gov/SP-4206/sp4206.html

lhttp://history.nasa.gov/gpo/order.html

NASA Systems Engineering Handbook, NASA SP-2007-6105.

If you enjoyed this book, you might also be interested in some of these.

16-bit Microprocessors, History and Architecture, 2013 PRRB Publishing, ISBN-1520210922.

4- and 8-bit Microprocessors, Architecture and History, 2013, PRRB Publishing, ISBN-152021572X,

Apollo's Computers, 2014, PRRB Publishing, ISBN-1520215800.

The Architecture and Applications of the ARM Microprocessors, 2013, PRRB Publishing, ISBN-1520215843.

Earth Rovers: for Exploration and Environmental Monitoring, 2014, PRRB Publishing, ISBN-152021586X.

Embedded Computer Systems, Volume 1, Introduction and Architecture, 2013, PRRB Publishing, ISBN-1520215959.

The History of Spacecraft Computers from the V-2 to the Space Station, 2013, PRRB Publishing, ISBN-1520216181.

Floating Point Computation, 2013, PRRB Publishing, ISBN-152021619X.

Architecture of Massively Parallel Microprocessor Systems, 2011, PRRB Publishing, ISBN-1520250061.

Multicore Computer Architecture, 2014, PRRB Publishing, ISBN-1520241372.

Personal Robots, 2014, PRRB Publishing, ISBN-1520216254.

RISC Microprocessors, History and Overview, 2013, PRRB Publishing, ISBN-1520216289.

*Robots and Telerobots in Space Application*s, 2011, PRRB Publishing, ISBN-1520210361.

The Saturn Rocket and the Pegasus Missions, 1965, 2013, PRRB Publishing, ISBN-1520209916.

Visiting the NASA Centers, and Locations of Historic Rockets & Spacecraft, 2017, PRRB Publishing, ISBN-1549651205.

Microprocessors in Space, 2011, PRRB Publishing, ISBN-1520216343.

Computer *Virtualization and the Cloud*, 2013, PRRB Publishing, ISBN-152021636X.

What's the Worst That Could Happen? Bad Assumptions, Ignorance, Failures and Screw-ups in Engineering Projects, 2014, PRRB Publishing, ISBN-1520207166.

Computer Architecture & Programming of the Intel x86 Family, 2013, PRRB Publishing, ISBN-1520263724.

The Hardware and Software Architecture of the Transputer, 2011,PRRB Publishing, ISBN-152020681X.

Mainframes, Computing on Big Iron, 2015, PRRB Publishing, ISBN- 1520216459.

Spacecraft Control Centers, 2015, PRRB Publishing, ISBN-1520200617.

Embedded in Space, 2015, PRRB Publishing, ISBN-1520215916.

A Practitioner's Guide to RISC Microprocessor Architecture, Wiley-Interscience, 1996, ISBN-0471130184.

Cubesat Engineering, PRRB Publishing, 2017, ISBN-1520754019.

Cubesat Operations, PRRB Publishing, 2017, ISBN-152076717X.

Interplanetary Cubesats, PRRB Publishing, 2017, ISBN-1520766173 .

Cubesat Constellations, Clusters, and Swarms, Stakem, PRRB Publishing, 2017, ISBN-1520767544.

Graphics Processing Units, an overview, 2017, PRRB Publishing, ISBN-1520879695.

Intel Embedded and the Arduino-101, 2017, PRRB Publishing, ISBN-1520879296.

Orbital Debris, the problem and the mitigation, 2018, PRRB Publishing, ISBN-*1980466483*.

Manufacturing in Space, 2018, PRRB Publishing, ISBN-1977076041.

NASA's Ships and Planes, 2018, PRRB Publishing, ISBN-1977076823.

Space Tourism, 2018, PRRB Publishing, ISBN-1977073506.

STEM – Data Storage and Communications, 2018, PRRB Publishing, ISBN-1977073115.

In-Space Robotic Repair and Servicing, 2018, PRRB Publishing, ISBN-1980478236.

Introducing Weather in the pre-K to 12 Curricula, A Resource Guide for Educators, 2017, PRRB Publishing, ISBN-1980638241.

Introducing Astronomy in the pre-K to 12 Curricula, A Resource Guide for Educators, 2017, PRRB Publishing, ISBN-198104065X.
Also available in a Brazilian Portuguese edition, ISBN-1983106127.

Deep Space Gateways, the Moon and Beyond, 2017, PRRB Publishing, ISBN-1973465701.

Exploration of the Gas Giants, Space Missions to Jupiter, Saturn, Uranus, and Neptune, PRRB Publishing, 2018, ISBN-9781717814500.

Crewed Spacecraft, 2017, PRRB Publishing, ISBN-1549992406.

Rocketplanes to Space, 2017, PRRB Publishing, ISBN-1549992589.

Crewed Space Stations, 2017, PRRB Publishing, ISBN-1549992228.

Enviro-bots for STEM: Using Robotics in the pre-K to 12 Curricula, A Resource Guide for Educators, 2017, PRRB Publishing, ISBN-1549656619.

STEM-Sat, Using Cubesats in the pre-K to 12 Curricula, A Resource Guide for Educators, 2017, ISBN-1549656376.

Embedded GPU's, 2018, PRRB Publishing, ISBN- 1980476497.

Mobile Cloud Robotics, 2018, PRRB Publishing, ISBN-1980488088.

Extreme Environment Embedded Systems, 2017, PRRB Publishing, ISBN-1520215967.

What's the Worst, Volume-2, 2018, ISBN-1981005579.

Spaceports, 2018, ISBN-1981022287.

Space Launch Vehicles, 2018, ISBN-1983071773.

Mars, 2018, ISBN-1983116902.

X-86, 40th Anniversary ed, 2018, ISBN-1983189405.

Lunar Orbital Platform-Gateway, 2018, PRRB Publishing, ISBN-1980498628.

Space Weather, 2018, ISBN-1723904023.

STEM-Engineering Process, 2017, ISBN-1983196517.

Space Telescopes, 2018, PRRB Publishing, ISBN-1728728568.

Exoplanets, 2018, PRRB Publishing, ISBN-9781731385055.

Planetary Defense, 2018, PRRB Publishing, ISBN-9781731001207.

Exploration of the Asteroid Belt, 2018, PRRB Publishing, ISBN-1731049846.

Terraforming, 2018, PRRB Publishing, ISBN-1790308100.

Martian Railroad, 2019, PRRB Publishing, ISBN-1794488243.

Exoplanets, 2019, PRRB Publishing, ISBN-1731385056.

Exploiting the Moon, 2019, PRRB Publishing, ISBN-1091057850.

RISC-V, an Open Source Solution for Space Flight Computers, 2019, PRRB Publishing, ISBN-1796434388.

Arm in Space, 2019, PRRB Publishing, ISBN-9781099789137.

Search for *Extraterrestrial Life*, 2019, PRRB Publishing, ISBN-978-1072072188.

Submarine Launched Ballistic Missiles, 2019, ISBN-978-1088954904.

Space Command, Military in Space, 2019, PRRB Publishing, ISBN-978-1693005398.

Robotic Exploration of the Icy moons of the Gas Giants, ISBN-979-8621431006.

History & Future of Cubesats, ISBN-978-1986536356.

Robotic Exploration of the Icy Moons of the Ice Giants, by Swarms of Cubesats, ISBN-979-8621431006.

Swarm Robotics, ISBN-979-8534505948.

Introduction to Electric Power Systems, ISBN-979-8519208727.

Powerships, Powerbarges, Floating Wind Farms: electricity when and where you need it, 2021, PRRB Publishing, ISBN-979-8716199477.

Centros de Control: Operaciones en Satélites del Estándar CubeSat (Spanish Edition), 2021, ISBN-979-8510113068.

The Artemis Missions, Return to the Moon, and on to Mars, 2021, ISBN-979-8490532361.

James Webb Space Telescope. A New Era in Astronomy, 2021, ISBN-979-8773857969.